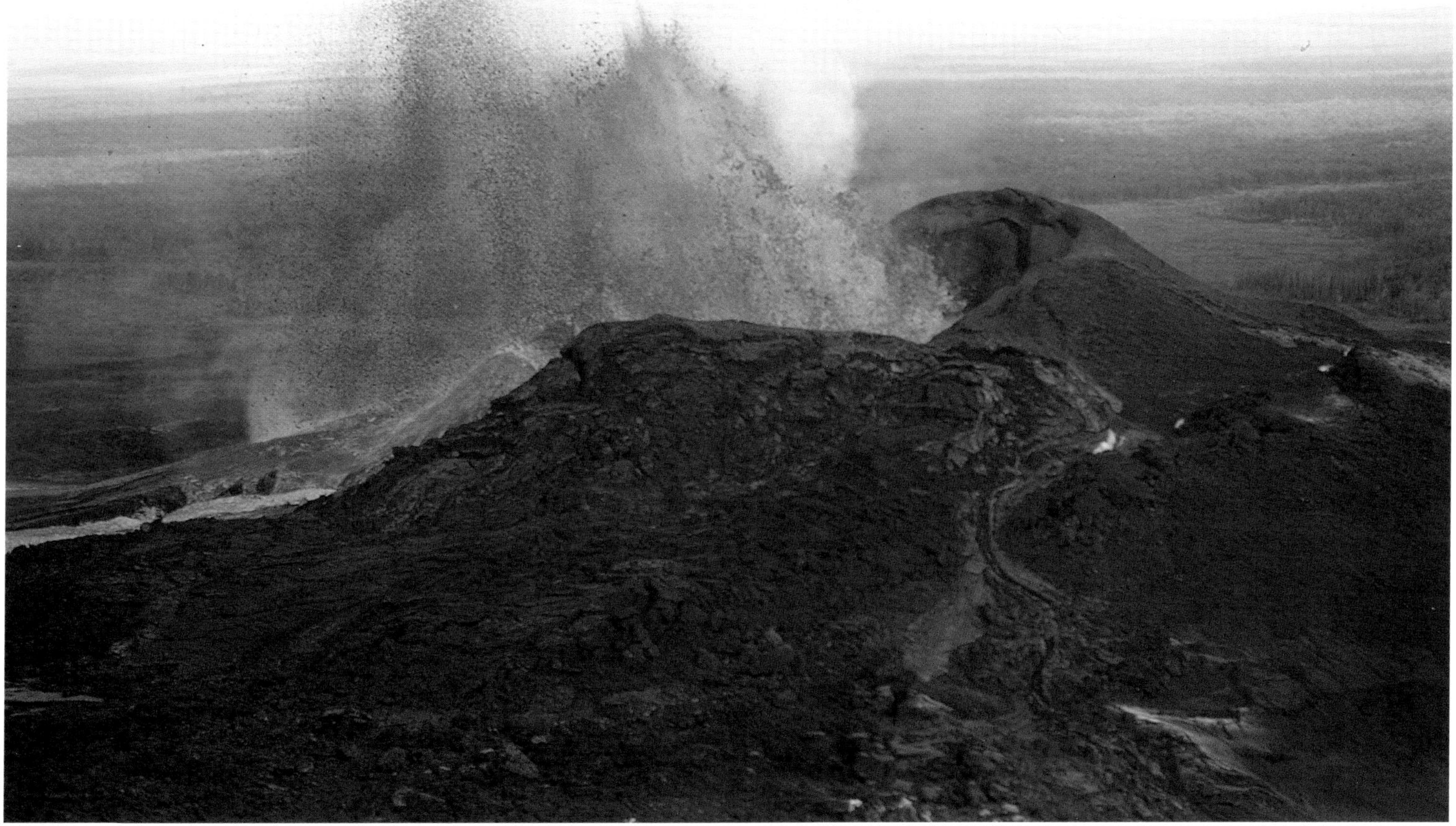

volcano

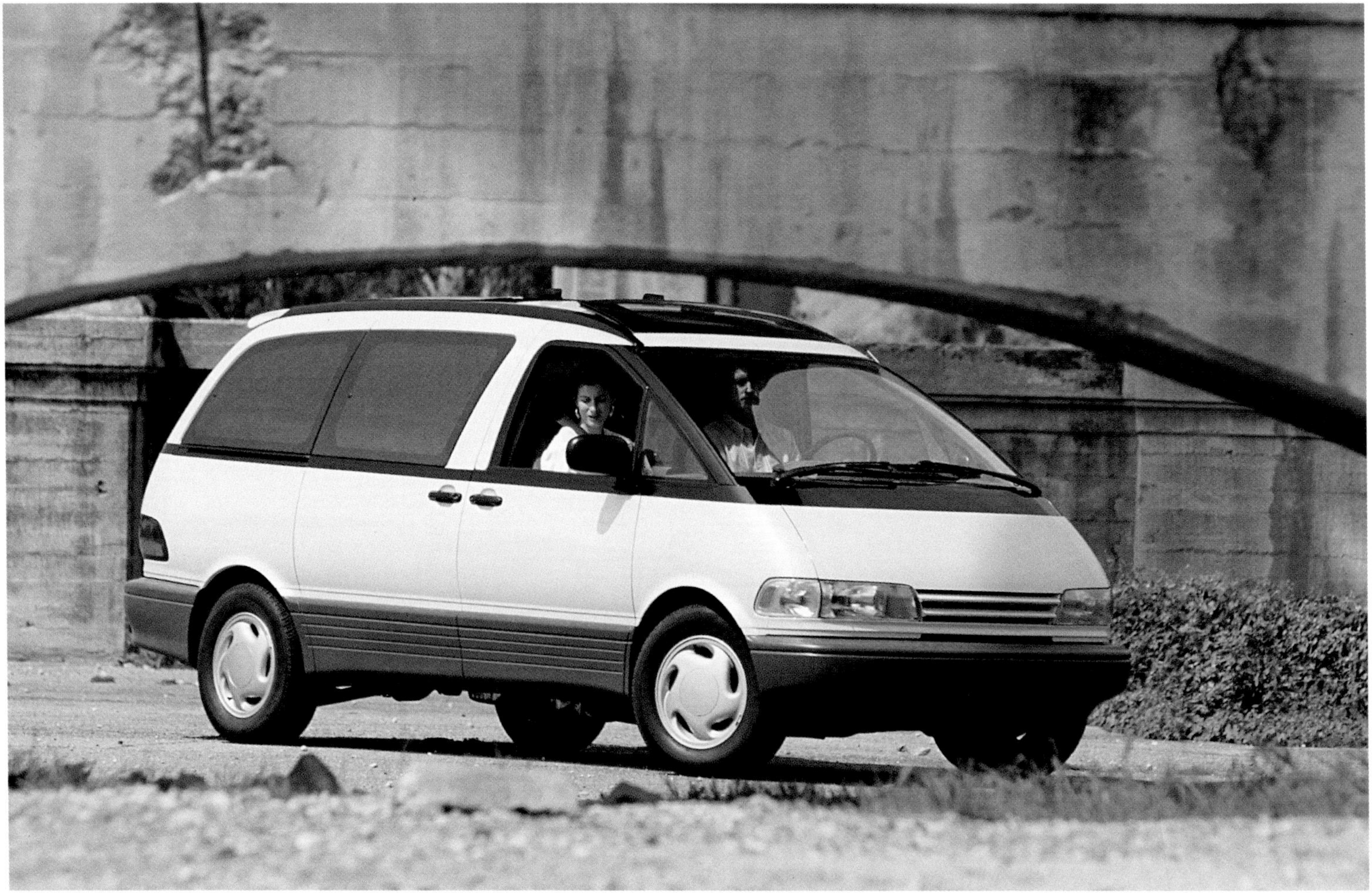

van

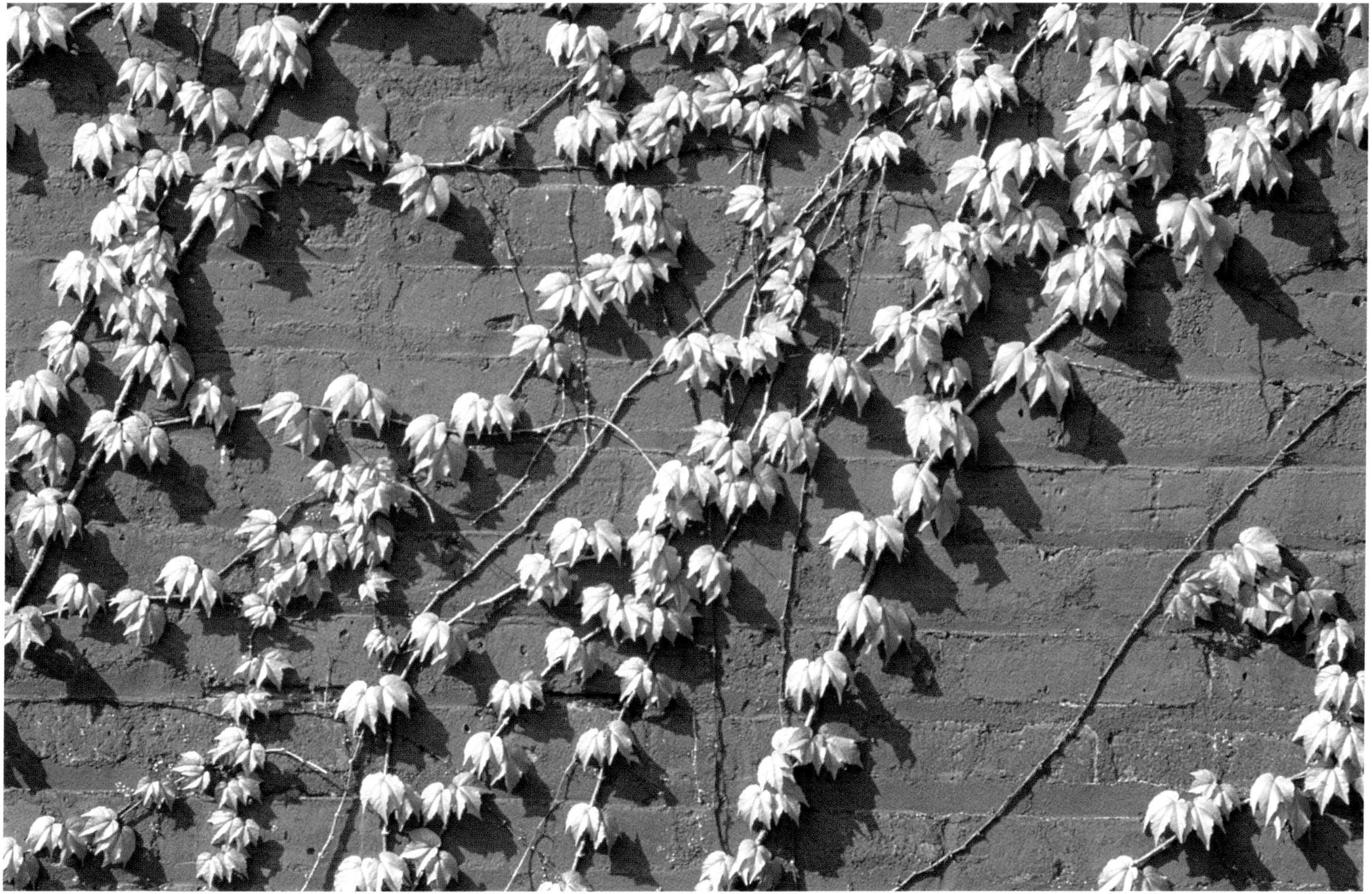

vine

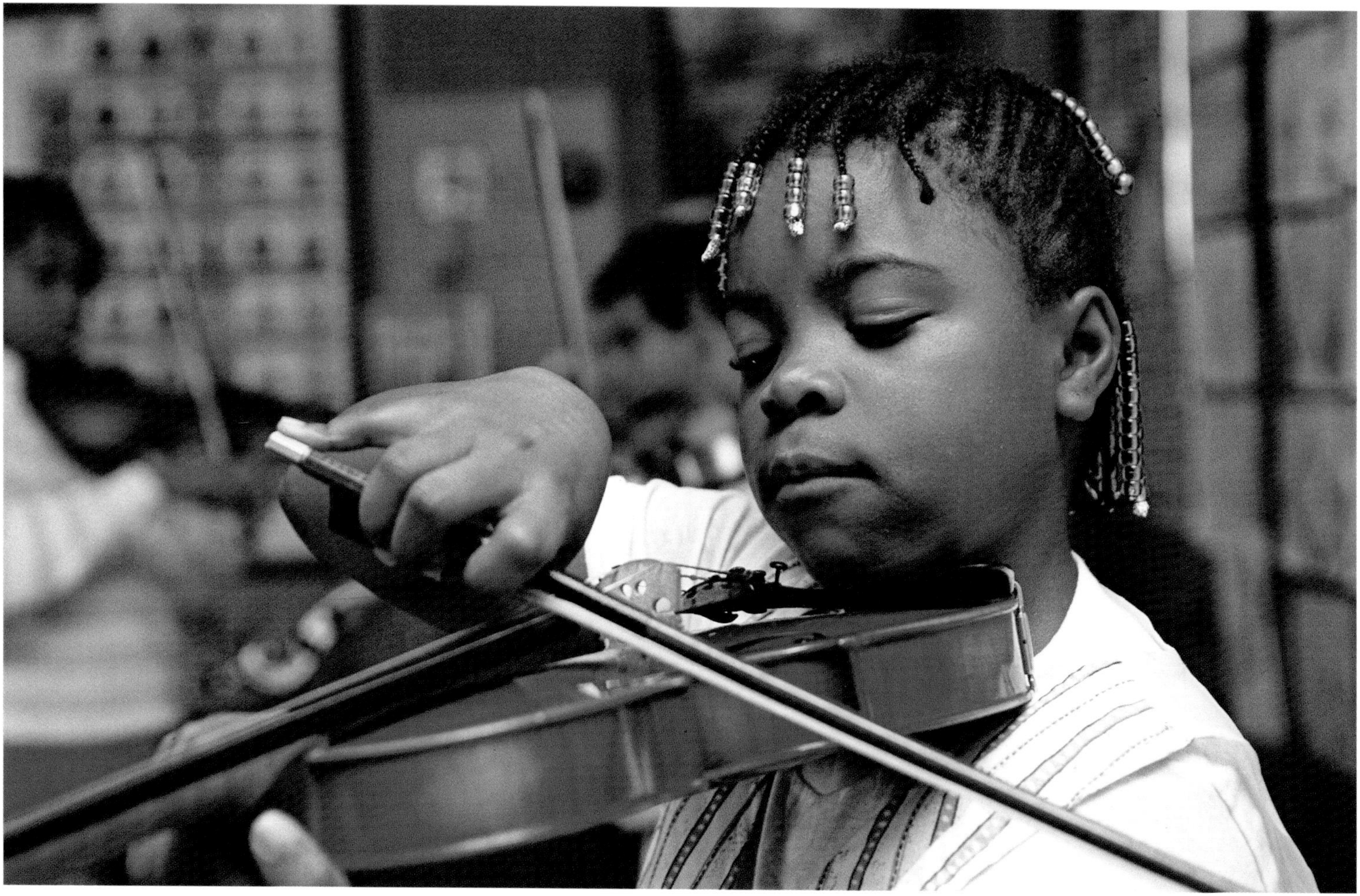

violin

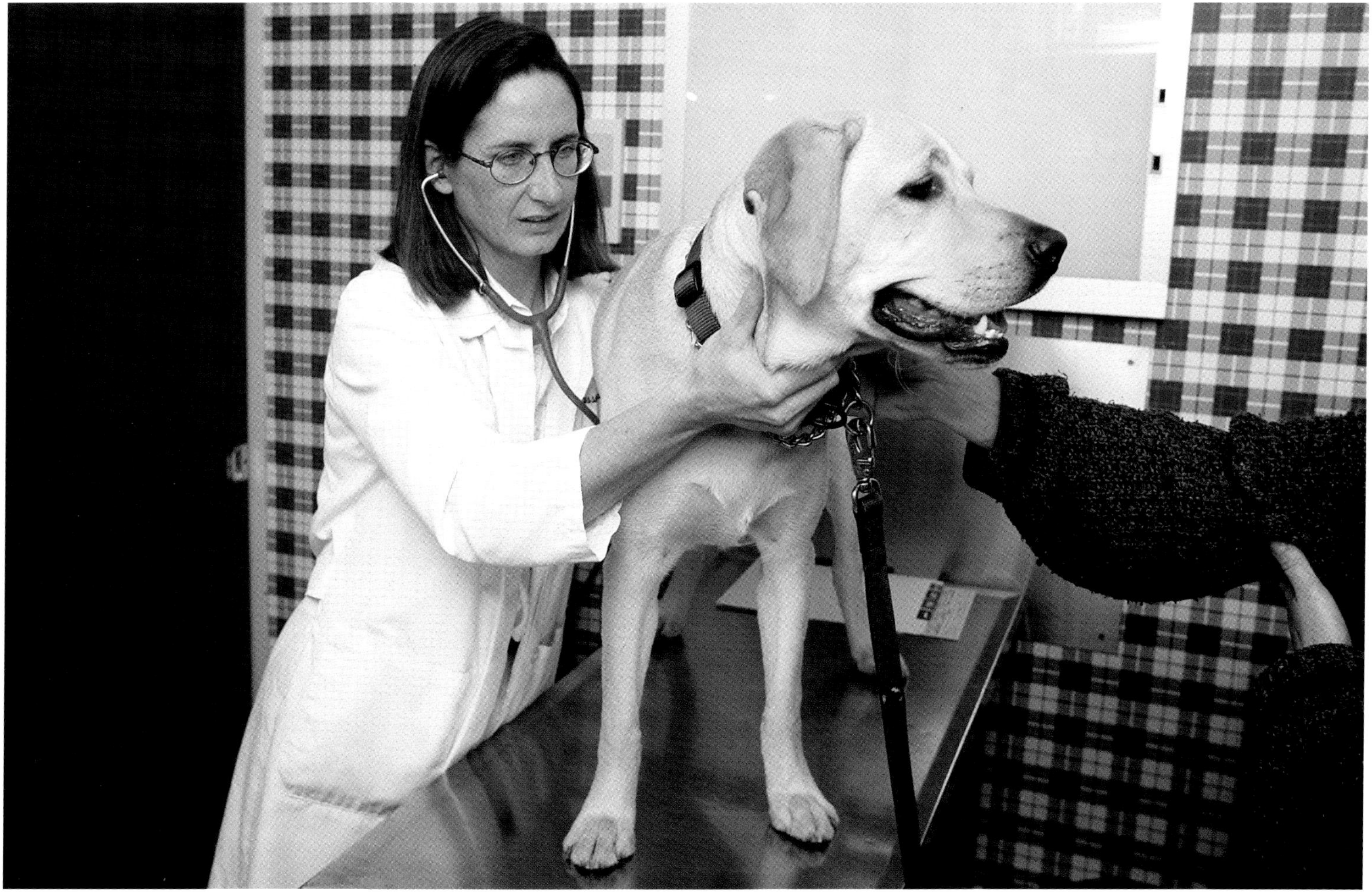

vet

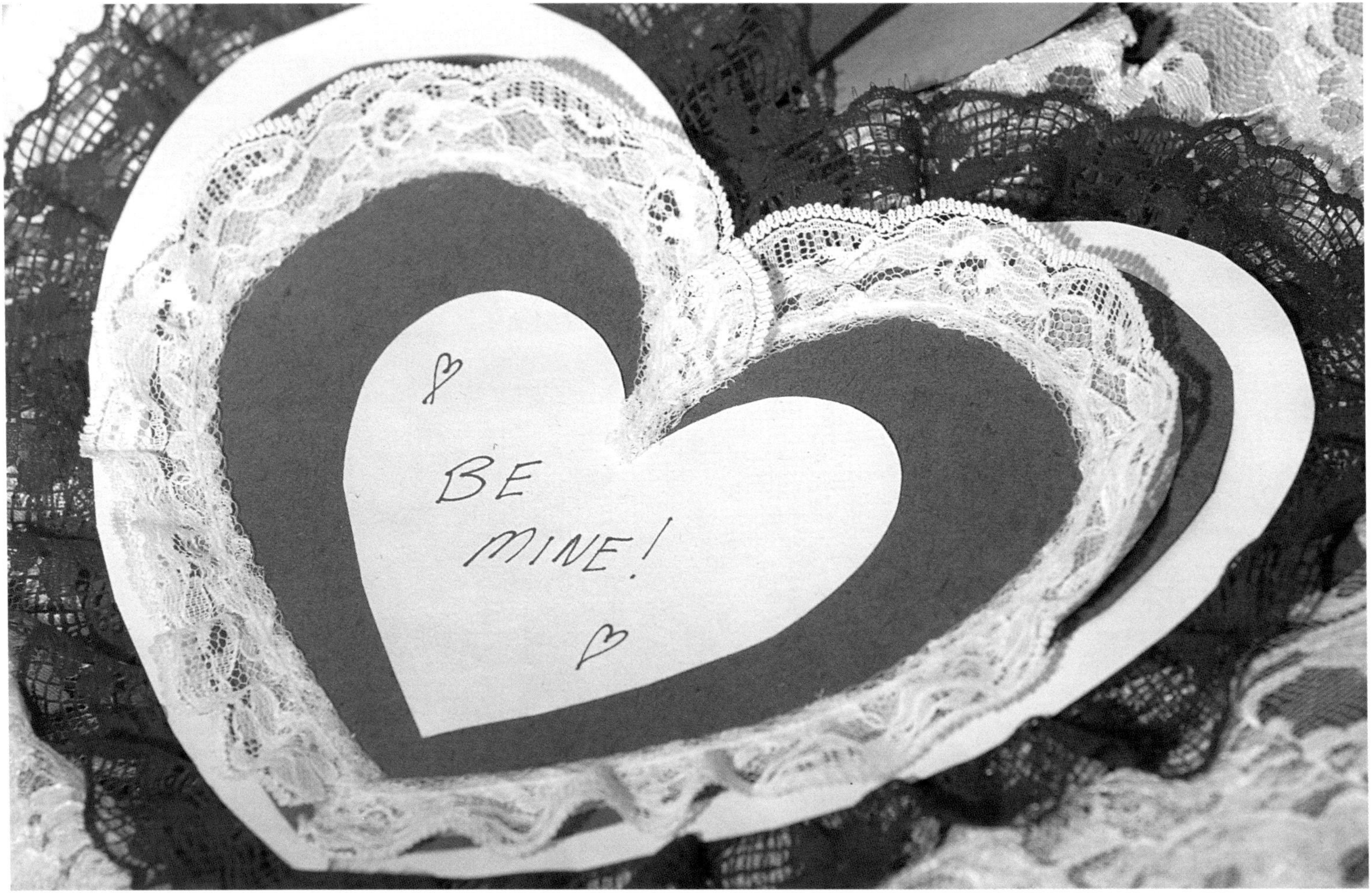

valentine

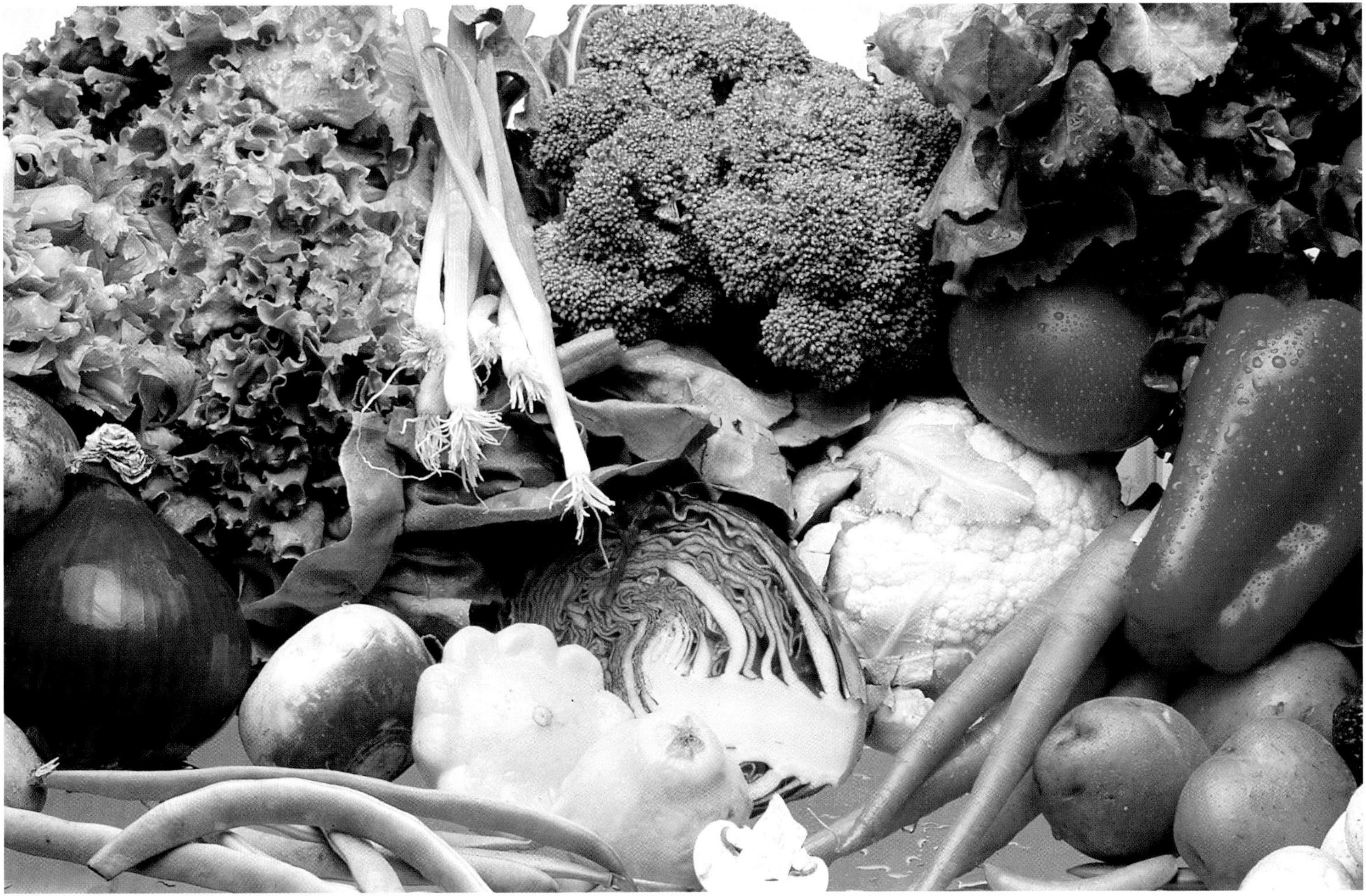

vegetables

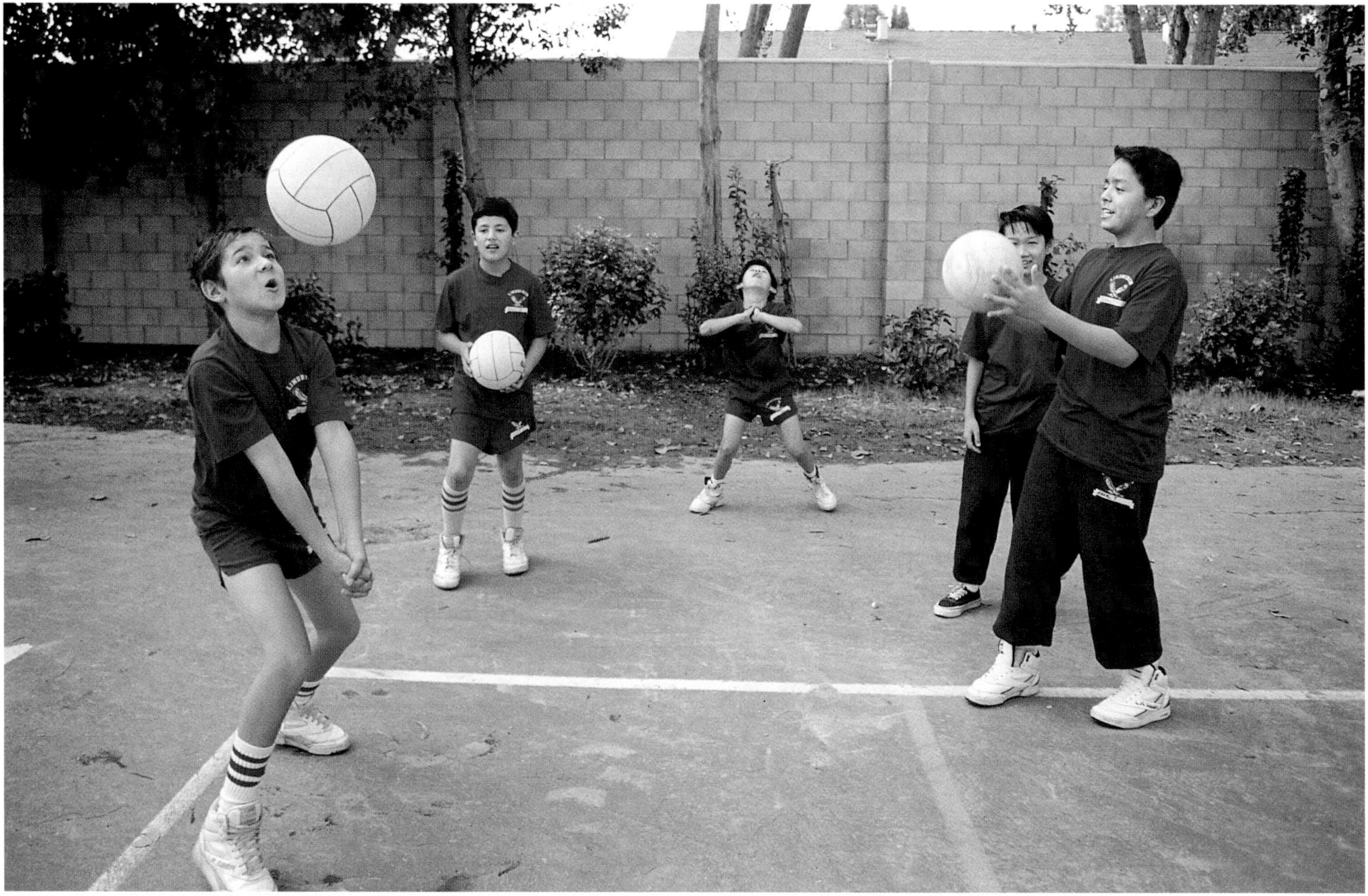

volleyball